CW00502487

Be What You Wish

Sublime Books
PO Box 632
Floyd Va 24091

ISBN-13: 978-1-5154-2284-6

FIRST EDITION

10 9 8 7 6 5 4 3 2 1

Be What You Wish

by Neville Goddard

Table of Contents

Be What You Wish

A newspaperman related to me that our great scientist, Robert Millikan, once told him that he had set a goal for himself at an early age when he was still very poor and unproven in the great work he was to do in the future. He condensed his dream of greatness and security into a simple statement, which statement, implied that his dream of greatness and security was already realized. Then he repeated the statement over and over again to himself until the idea of greatness and security filled his mind and crowded all other ideas out of his consciousness. These may not have been the words of Dr. Millikan but they are those given to me and I quote, "I have a lavish, steady, dependable income, consistent with integrity and mutual benefit." As I have said repeatedly, everything depends upon our attitude towards ourselves. That which we will not affirm as true of ourselves cannot develop in our life. Dr. Millikan wrote his dream of greatness and security in the first person, present tense. He did not say, "I will be great; I will be secure," for that would have implied that he was not great and secure. Instead, he made his future dream a present fact. "I have," said he, "a lavish, steady, dependable income, consistent with integrity and mutual benefit."

The future dream must become a present fact in the mind of him who seeks to realize it. We must experience in imagination what we would experience in reality in the event we achieved our goal, for the soul imagining itself into a situation takes on the results of that imaginary act. If it does not imagine itself into a situation, it is ever free of the result.

It is the purpose of this teaching to lift us to a higher state of consciousness, to stir the highest in us to confidence and self-assertion, for that which stirs the highest in us is our teacher and healer. The very first word of correction or cure is always, "Arise." If we are to understand the reason for this constant command of the Bible to "arise," we must recognize that the universe understood internally is an infinite series of levels and man is what he is according to where he is in that series. As we are lifted up in consciousness, our world reshapes itself in harmony with the level to which we are lifted. He who rises from his prayer a better man, his prayer has been granted.

To change the present state we, like Dr. Millikan, must rise to a higher level of consciousness. This rise is accomplished by affirming that we are already that which we want to be; by assuming the feeling of the wish fulfilled. The drama of life is a psychological one which we bring to pass by our attitudes rather than by our acts. There is no escape from our present predicament except by a radical psychological transformation. Everything depends upon our attitude towards ourselves. That which we will not affirm as true of ourselves will not develop in our lives.

We hear much of the humble man, the meek man – but what is meant by a meek man? He is not poor and groveling, the proverbial doormat, as he is generally conceived to be. Men who make themselves as worms in their own sight have lost the vision of that life – into the likeness of which it is the true purpose of the spirit to transform this life. Men should take their measurements not from life as they see it but from men like Dr. Millkan, who, while poor and unproven, dared to assume, "I have a lavish, steady, dependable income, consistent with integrity and mutual benefit." Such men are the meek of the Gospels, the men who inherit the earth. Any concept of self less than the best robs us of the earth. The promise is, "Blessed are the meek, for they shall inherit the earth." In the original text, the word translated as meek is the opposite of the words – resentful – angry. It has the meaning of becoming "tamed" as a wild animal is tamed. After the mind is tamed, it may be likened to a vine, of which it may be said, "Behold this vine. I found it a wild tree whose wanton strength had swollen into irregular twigs. But I pruned the plant, and it grew temperate in its vain expense of useless leaves, and knotted as you see into these clean, full clusters to repay the hand that wisely wounded it."

A meek man is a self-disciplined man. He is so disciplined he sees only the finest, he thinks only the best. He is the one who fulfills the suggestion, "Brethren, whatsoever things are true, whatsoever things are honest, whatsoever things are just, whatsoever things are pure, whatsoever things are lovely, whatsoever things are of good report; if there be any virtue and if there be any praise, think on these things."

We rise to a higher level of consciousness, not because we have curbed our passions, but because we have cultivated our virtues. In truth, a meek man is a man in complete control of his moods, and his moods are the highest, for he knows he must keep a high mood if he would walk with the highest.

It is my belief that all men can, like Dr. Millikan, change the course of their lives. I believe that Dr. Millikan's technique of making his desire a present fact to himself is of great importance to any seeker after the "truth." It is also his high purpose to be of "mutual benefit" that is inevitably the goal of us all. It is much easier to imagine the good of all than to be purely selfish in our imagining. By our imagination, by our affirmations, we can change our world, we can change our future. To the man of high purpose, to the disciplined man, this is a natural measure, so let us all become disciplined men. Next Sunday morning, July 15th, I am speaking as the guest of Dr. Bailes at 10:30 at the Fox-Wilshire Theater on Wilshire Boulevard, near La Cienega. My subject for next Sunday is "Changing Your Future." It is a subject near to the hearts of us all. I hope you will all come on Sunday to learn how to be the disciplined man, the meek man, who "changes his future" to the benefit of his fellow man. If you are observant, you will notice the swift echo or response to your every mood in this message and you will be able to key it to the circumstances of your daily life. When we are certain of the relationship of mood to circumstance in our lives, we welcome what befalls us. We know that all we meet is part of ourselves. In the creation of a new life we must begin at the beginning, with a change of mood. Every high mood of man is the opening of the door to a higher level for him. Let us mold our lives about a high mood or a community of high moods. Individuals, as well as communities, grow spiritually in proportion as they rise to a higher ideal. If their ideal is lowered, they sink to its depths; if their ideal is exalted, they are elevated to heights unimagined. We must keep the high mood if we would walk with the highest; the heights, also, were meant for habitation. All forms of the creative imagination imply elements of feeling. Feeling is the ferment without which no creation is possible. There is nothing wrong with our desire to transcend our present state. There would be no progress in this world were it not for man's dissatisfaction with himself. It is natural for us to seek a more beautiful personal life; it is right that we wish for greater understanding, greater health, greater security. It is stated in the sixteenth chapter of the Gospel of

St. John, "Heretofore have ye asked for nothing in my name; ask and ye shall receive, that your joy may be full."

A spiritual revival is needed for mankind, but by spiritual revival I mean a true religious attitude, one in which each individual, himself, accepts the challenge of embodying a new and higher value of himself as Dr. Millikan did. A nation can exhibit no greater wisdom in the mass than it generates in its units. For this reason, I have always preached self-help, knowing that if we strive passionately after this kind of self-help, that is, to embody a new and higher concept of ourselves, then all other kinds of help will be at our service.

The ideal we serve and hope to achieve is ready for a new incarnation; but unless we offer it human parentage it is incapable of birth. We must affirm that we are already that which we hope to be and live as though we were, knowing like Dr. Millikan, that our assumption, though false to the outer world, if persisted in, will harden into fact.

The perfect man judges not after appearances; he judges righteously. He sees himself and others as he desires himself and them to be. He hears what he wants to hear. He sees and hears only the good. He knows the truth, and the truth sets him free and leads him to good. The truth shall set all mankind free. This is our spiritual revival. Character is largely the result of the direction and persistence of voluntary attention.

"Think truly, and thy thoughts shall the world's famine feed;
Speak truly, and each word of thine shall be a fruitful seed;
Live truly, and thy life shall be a great and noble creed."

How to Use Your Imagina

The purpose of this record is to show you how to use your imagination to achieve your every desire. Most men are totally unaware of the creative power of imagination and invariably bow before the dictates of "facts" and accepts life on the basis of the world without. But when you discover this creative power within yourself, you will boldly assert the supremacy of imagination and put all things in subjection to it. When a man speaks of God-in-man, he is totally unaware that this power called God-in-man is man's imagination. THIS is the creative power in man. There is nothing under heaven that is not plastic as potter's clay to the touch of the shaping spirit of imagination.

Once a man said to me, "You know, Neville, I love to listen to you talk about imagination, but as I do so, I invariably touch the chair with my fingers and push my feet into the rug just to keep my sense of the reality and the profundity of things. Well, undoubtedly he is still touching the chair with his fingers and pushing his feet into the rug.

Well, let me tell you of another one who didn't touch with her fingers and didn't push that foot of hers onto the board of the streetcar. It's the story of a young girl just turned seventeen. It was Christmas Eve, and she is sad of heart, for that year she had lost her father in an accident, and she is returning home to what seemed to be an empty house. She was untrained to do anything, so got herself a job as a waitress. This night it's quite late, Christmas Eve, it's raining, the car is full of laughing boys and girls home for their Christmas vacation, and she couldn't conceal the tears.

Luckily for her, as I said, it was raining, so she stuck her face into the heavens to mingle her tears with rain. And then holding the rail of the streetcar, this is what she did: she said, "This is not rain, why, this is spray from the ocean; and this is not the salt of tears that I taste, for this is the salt of the sea in the wind; and this is not San Diego, this is a ship, and I am coming into the Bay of Samoa." And there she felt the reality of all that she had imagined.

Be What You Wish

Then came the end of the journey and all are out.

Ten days later this girl received a letter from a firm in Chicago saying that her aunt, several years before when she sailed for Europe, deposited with them three thousand dollars with instructions that if she did not return to America, this money should be paid to her niece. They had just received information of the aunt's death and were now acting upon her instructions. One month later this girl sailed for Samoa. As she came into the bay it was late that night and there was salt of the sea in the wind. It wasn't raining, but there was spray in the air. And she actually felt what she'd felt one month before, only this time she had realized her objective.

Now, this whole record is technique. I want to show you today how to put your wonderful imagination right into the feeling of your wish fulfilled and let it remain there and fall asleep in that state. And I promise you, from my own experience, you will realize the state in which you sleep - if you could actually feel yourself right into the situation of your fulfilled desire and continue therein until you fall asleep. As you feel yourself right into it, remain in it until you give it all the tones of reality, until you give it all the sensory vividness of reality. As you do it, in that state, quietly fall into sleep. And in a way you will never know - you could never consciously devise the means that would be employed - you will find yourself moving across a series of events leading you towards the objective realization of this state.

Now, here is a practical technique: The first thing you do, you must know exactly what you want in this world. When you know exactly what you want, make as life-like a representation as possible of what you would see, and what you would touch, and what you would do were you physically present and physically moving in such a state.

For example, suppose I wanted a home, but I had no money - but I still know what I want. I, without taking anything into consideration, I would make as life-like a representation of the home that I would like, with all the things in it that I would want. And then, this night, as I would go to bed, I would in a state, a drowsy, sleepy state, the state that borders upon sleep, I would imagine that I am actually in such a house, that were I to step off the bed, I would step upon the floor of that house, were I to leave this room, I would enter the room that is adjacent to my imagined room in that house. And while I am touching the furniture and feeling it to be solidly real, and while I am moving from one room to the other in my imaginary house, I would go to sound asleep in that state. And I know that in a way I could not consciously devise, I would realize my house. I have seen it work time and time again.

If I wanted promotion in my business I would ask myself, "What additional responsibilities would be mine were I to be given this great promotion? What would I do? What would I say? What would I see? How would I act? And then in my imagination I would begin to see and touch and do and act as I would outwardly see and touch and act were I in that position.

If I now desired the mate of my life, were I now in search of some wonderful girl or some wonderful man, what would I actually find myself doing that would imply that I have found my state? For instance, suppose now I was a lady, one thing I would definitely do, I would wear a wedding ring. I would take my imaginary hands and I would feel the ring that I would imagine to be there. And I would keep on feeling it and feeling it until it seemed to me to be solidly real. I would give it all the sensory vividness I am capable of giving anything. And while I am feeling my imaginary ring - which implies that I am married - I would sleep.

This story is told us in The Song of Songs, or A Song of Solomon:

It is said, "At night on my bed I sought him whom my soul loveth. I found him whom my soul loveth, and I would not let him go until I had brought him into my mother's house, right into the chamber of her that conceived me." If I would take that beautiful poem and put it into modern English, into practical language, it would be this: "While sitting in my chair I would feel myself right into the situation of my fulfilled desire, and having felt myself into that state I would not let it go. I would keep that mood alive, and in that mood I would sleep." That is taking it "right into my mother's chamber, into the chamber of her that conceived me."

You know, people are totally unaware of this fantastic power of the imagination, but when man begins to discover this power within him, he never plays the part that he formerly played. He doesn't turn back and become just a reflector of life; from here on in he is the affector of life. The secret of it is to center your imagination in the feeling of the wish fulfilled and remain therein. For in our capacity to live IN the feeling of the wish fulfilled lies our capacity to live the more abundant life. Most of us are afraid to imagine ourselves as important and noble individuals secure in our contribution to the world just because, at the very moment that we start our assumption, reason and our senses deny the truth of our assumption. We seem to be in the grip of an unconscious urge which makes us cling desperately to the world of familiar things and resist all that threatens to tear us away from our familiar and seemingly safe moorings.

Well, I appeal to you to try it. If you try it, you will discover this great wisdom of the ancients. For they told it to us in their own strange, wonderful, symbolical form. But unfortunately you and I misinterpreted their stories and took it for history, when they intended it as instruction to simply achieve our every objective. You see, imagination puts us inwardly in touch with the world of states. These states are existent, they are present now, but they are mere possibilities while we think OF them. But they become overpoweringly real when we think FROM them and dwell IN them.

You know, there is a wide difference between thinking OF what you want in this world and thinking FROM what you want. Let me tell you when I first heard of this strange and wonderful power of the imagination. It was in 1933 in New York City. An old friend of mine taught it to me.

He turned to the fourteenth of John, and this is what he read: "In my father's house are many mansions. If it were not so, I would have told you. I go to prepare a place for you, and if I go and prepare a place for you, I will come again and receive you unto myself, that where I am there ye may be also." He explained to me that this central character of the Gospels was human imagination; that 'mansion' was not a place in some heavenly house, but simply my desire. If I would make a living representation of the state desired and then enter that state and abide in that state, I would realize it.

At the time I wanted to make a trip to the island of Barbados in the

West Indies, but I had no money. He explained to me that if I would that night, as I slept in New York City, assume that I was sleeping in my earthly father's house in Barbados and go sound asleep in that state, that I would realize my trip. Well, I took him at his word and tried it. For one month, night after night as I fell asleep I assumed I was sleeping in my father's home in Barbados. At the end of my month an invitation from my family came inviting me to spend the winter in Barbados. I sailed for Barbados the early part of December of that year.

From then on I knew I had found this savior in myself. The old man told me that it would never fail. Even after it happened I could hardly believe that it would not have happened anyway. That's how strange this whole thing is. On reflection, it happens so naturally you begin to feel or to tell yourself, "Well, it would have happened anyway," and you quickly recover from this wonderful experience of yours.

It never failed me if I would give the mood, the imagined mood, sensory vividness. I could tell you unnumbered case histories to show you how it works, but in essence it is simple: You simply know what you want. When you know what you want, you are thinking of it. That is not enough. You must now begin to think FROM it. Well, how could I think from it? I am sitting here, and I desire to be elsewhere. How could I, while sitting here physically, put myself in imagination at a point in space removed from this room and make that real to me?

Quite easily. My imagination puts me in touch inwardly with that state. I imagine that I am actually where I desire to be. How can I tell that I am there? There is one way to prove that I am there, for what a man sees when he describes his world is, as he describes it, relative to himself. So what the world looks like depends entirely upon where I stand when I make my observation. So, if as I describe my world it is related to that point in space I imagine that I am occupying, then I must be there. I am not there physically, no, but I AM there in my imagination, and my imagination is my real self! And where I go in imagination and make it real, there I shall go in the flesh, also. When in that state I fall asleep, it is done. I have never seen it fail. So this is the simple technique upon how to use your imagination to realize your every objective.

Here is a very healthy and productive exercise for the imagination, something that you should do daily: Daily relive the day as you wish you had lived it, revising the scenes to make them conform to your ideals. For instance, suppose today's mail brought disappointing news. Revise the letter. Mentally rewrite it and make it conform to the news you wish you had received. Or, suppose you didn't get the letter you wish you had received. Write yourself the letter and imagine that you received such a letter.

Let me tell you a story that took place in New York not very long ago. In my audience sat this lady who had heard me, oh, numerous times, and I was telling the story of revision - that man, not knowing the power of imagination, he goes to sleep at the end of his day, tired and exhausted, accepting as final all the events of the day. And I was trying to show that man should, at that moment before he sleeps, he should rewrite the entire day and make it conform to the day he wished he had experienced.

Here is the way a lady wisely used this law of revision: It appears that two years ago she was ordered out of her daughter-in-law's home. For two years there was no correspondence. She had sent her grandson at least two dozen presents in that interval, but not one was ever acknowledged. Having heard the story of revision, this is what she did: As she retired at night, she mentally constructed two letters, one she imagined coming from her grandson, and the other from her daughter-in-law. In these letters they expressed deep affection for her and wondered why she had not called to see them.

This she did for seven consecutive nights, holding in her imaginary hand the letter she imagined she had received and reading these letters over and over until it aroused within her the satisfaction of having heard. Then she slept. On the eighth day she received a letter from her daughter-in-law. On the inside there were two letters, one from her grandson and one from the daughter-in-law. They practically duplicated the imaginary letters that this grandmother had written to herself eight days before.

This art of revision can be used in any department of your life. Take the matter of health. Suppose you were ill. Bring before your mind's eye the image of a friend. Put upon that face an expression which implies that he or she sees in you that which you want the whole world to see. Just imagine he is saying to you that he has never seen you look better, and you reply, "I have never felt better."

Suppose your foot was injured. Then do this: Construct mentally a drama which implies that you are walking - that you are doing all the things that you would do if the foot was normal, and do it over and over and over until it takes on the tones of reality. Whenever you do in your imagination that which you would like to do in the outer world, that you WILL do in the outer world.

The one requisite is to arouse your attention in a way, and to such intensity, that you become wholly absorbed in the revised action. You will experience an expansion and refinement of the senses by this imaginative exercise and, eventually, achieve vision in the inner world. The abundant life promised us is ours to enjoy now, but not until we have the sense of the creator as our imagination can we experience it.

Persistent imagination, centered in the feeling of the wish fulfilled, is the secret of all successful operations. This alone is the means of fulfilling the intention.

Every stage of man's progress is made by the conscious, voluntary exercise of the imagination. Then you will understand why all poets have stressed the importance of controlled, vivid imagination.

Listen to this one by the great William Blake:
"In your own bosom you bear your heaven and earth,
And all you behold, though it appears without,
It is within, in your imagination,
Of which this world of mortality is but a shadow."

Try it, and you too will prove that your Imagination is the Creator.

Mental Diets

Talking to oneself is a habit everyone indulges in. We could no more stop talking to ourselves than we could stop eating and drinking. All that we can do is control the nature and the direction of our inner conversations. Most of us are totally unaware of the fact that our inner conversations are the causes of the circumstance of our life.

We are told that "as a man thinketh in his heart, so is he." But do we know that man's thinking follows the tracks laid down in his own inner conversations? To turn the tracks to which he is tied in the direction in which he wants to go, he must put off his former conversation, which is called in the Bible the Old Man, and be renewed in the spirit of his mind. Speech is the image of mind; therefore, to change his mind, he must first change his speech. By 'speech' is meant those mental conversations we carry on with ourselves.

The world is a magic circle of infinite possible mental transformations. For there are an infinite number of possible mental conversations. When man discovers the creative power of inner talking, he will realize his function and his mission in life. Then he can act to a purpose. Without such knowledge, he acts unconsciously. Everything is a manifestation of the mental conversations which go on in us without our being aware of them. But as civilized beings, we must become aware of them and act with a purpose.

A man's mental conversations attracts his life. As long as there is no change in his inner talking, the personal history of the man remains the same. To attempt to change the world before we change our inner talking is to struggle against the very nature of things. Man can go round and round in the same circle of disappointments and misfortunes, not seeing them as caused by his own negative inner talking, but as caused by others.

This may seem far-fetched, but it is a matter which lends itself to research and experiment. The formula the chemist illustrates is not more certainly provable than the formula of this science by which words are clothed in objective reality.

One day a girl told me of her difficulties in working with her employer. She was convinced that he unjustly criticized and rejected her very best efforts. Upon hearing her story, I explained that if she thought him unfair, it was a suresign that she herself was in need of a new conversation piece. There was no doubt but that she was mentally arguing with her employer, for others only echo that which we whisper to them in secret.

She confessed that she argued mentally with him all day long. When she realized what she had been doing, she agreed to change her inner conversations with her employer. She imagined that he had congratulated her on her fine work, and that she in turn had thanked him for his praise and kindness. To her great delight, she soon discovered that her own attitude was the cause of all that befell her. The behavior of her employer reversed itself. It echoed, as it had always done, her mental conversations with him.

I rarely see a person alone without wondering, "to what conversation piece is he tied? On what mysterious track is he walking?" We must begin to take life consciously. For the solution of all problems lies just in this: the Second Man, the Lord from heaven in all of us, is trying to become self-conscious in the body, that he may be about his father's business. What are his labors? To imitate his father, to become master of the Word, master of his inner talking, that he may mold this world of ours into a likeness with the Kingdom of Love.

The prophet said, "Be ye imitators of God as dear children." How would I imitate God? Well, we are told that God calls things that are not seen as though they were seen, and the unseen becomes seen. This is the way the girl called forth praise and kindness from her employer. She carried on an imaginary conversation with her employer from the premise that he had praised her work, and he did.

Our inner conversations represent in various ways the world we live in. Our individual worlds are self-revelations of our own inner speech. We are told that every idle word that men shall speak they shall give account thereof. For by their words they shall be justified, and by their words they shall be condemned.

We abandon ourselves to negative inner talking, yet expect to retain command of life. Our present mental conversations do not recede into the past as man believes. They advance into the future to confront us as wasted or invested words. "My Word," said the prophet, "shall not return unto me void, but it shall accomplish that which I please, and it shall prosper in all the things whereto I sent it."

How would I send my Word to help a friend? I would imagine that I am hearing his voice, that he is physically present, that my hand is on him. I would then congratulate him on his good fortune, tell him that I have never seen him look better. I would listen as though I heard him; I would imagine that he is telling me he has never felt better, he has never been happier. And I would know that in this loving, knowing communion with another, a communion populous with loving thoughts and feelings, that my word was sent, and it shall not return unto me void, but it shall prosper in the thing whereto I sent it.

"Now is the accepted time, now is the day of salvation." It is only what is done now that counts, even though its effects may not be visible until tomorrow. We call, not out loud, but by an inner effort of intense attention; to listen attentively, as though you heard, is to create. The events and relationships of life are your Word made visible. Most of us rob others of their willingness and their ability to be kind and generous by our fixed attitudes towards them.

Our attitudes unfold within us in the form of mental conversations. Inner talking from premises of fulfilled desire is the way to consciously create circumstances.

Our inner conversations are perpetually out-pictured all around us in happenings. Therefore, what we desire to see and hear without we must see and hear within, for the whole manifested world goes to show us what use we have made of the Word.

If you practice this art of controlled inner speaking, you too will know what a thrill it is to be able to say, "And now I have told you before it come to pass, that when it is come to pass, ye might believe." You will be able to consciously use your imagination to transform and channel the immense creative energies of your inner speech from the mental, emotional level to the physical level. And I do not know what limits, if any, there are to such a process.

What is your aim? Does your inner talking match it? It must, you know, if you would realize your aim. For as the prophet asked, "Can two walk together except they be agreed?" And of course the answer is, "No, they cannot." The two who must agree are your inner conversation and the state desired. That is, what you desire to see and hear without, you must see and hear within.

Every stage of man's progress is made by the conscious exercise of his imagination matching his inner speech to his fulfilled desire. As we control our inner talking, matching it to our fulfilled desires, we can lay aside all other processes. Then we simply act by clear imagination and intention: we imagine the wish fulfilled and carry on mental conversations from that premise. The right inner speech is the speech that would be yours were you to realize your ideal. In other words, it is the speech of fulfilled desire.

Now you will understand how wise the ancient was when he told us in the Hermetica, "There are two gifts which God has bestowed upon man alone and on no other mortal creature. These two are Mind and Speech, and the gift of Mind and Speech is equivalent to that of immortality. If a man uses these two gifts rightly, he will differ in nothing from the Immortals. And when he quits his body, Mind and Speech will be his guides, and by them he will be brought into the troop of the gods and the souls that have attained to bliss."

With the gift of Mind and Speech you create the conditions and circumstances of life. "In the beginning was the Word, and the Word was with God, and the Word was God." The Word, said Hermes, is Son, and Mind is Father of the Word. They are not separate one from the other, for life is the union of Word and Mind. You and your inner talking, or Word, are one. If your mind is one with your inner conversations, then to be transformed in mind is to be transformed in conversation.

It was a flash of the deepest insight that taught Paul to write:

"Put off the former conversation, the Old Man which is corrupt, and be renewed

in the spirit of your mind. Put on the New Man." "Put on the New Man," and "be

renewed in the spirit of your mind," is to change your inner conversation, for

speech and mind are one - a change of speech is a change of mind.

The prophet Samuel said, "The Lord spake by me, and his Word was in my tongue." If the Lord's Word was in the prophet's tongue, then the Lord's mouth that uttered the Word must be the prophet's mind, for inner conversations originate in the mind and produce little tiny speech movements in the tongue. The prophet is telling us that the mouth of God is the mind of man, that our inner conversations are the Word of God creating life about us as we create it within ourselves.

In the Bible you are told that the Word is very near to you, in your mouth and in your heart, that you may do it.

"See, I have set before you this day life and good, death and evil, blessings and cursings. Choose life."

The conditions and circumstances of life are not created by some power external to yourself; they are the conditions which result from the exercise of your freedom of choice, your freedom to choose the ideas to which you will respond.

Now is the accepted time. This is the day of salvation. Whatsoever things are of good report, think on these things. For your future will be formed by the Word of God which is your present inner talking. You create your future by your inner conversations. The worlds were framed by the Word of God, that is, your inner talking.

See yonder fields? The sesamum was sesamum, the corn was corn. The silence and the darkness knew! So is a man's fate born. (The Light of Asia)

For ends run true to origins. If you would reap success, you must plant success. The idea in your mind which starts the whole process going is the idea which you accept as truth. This is a very important point to grasp, for truth depends upon the intensity of imagination, not upon "facts." When the girl imagined that her employer was unfair, his behavior confirmed her imagination. When she changed her assumption of him, his behavior reflected the change, proving that an assumption, though false, if persisted in will harden into fact.

The mind always behaves according to the assumption with which it starts. Therefore, to experience success, we must assume that we are successful. We must live wholly on the level of the imagination itself, and it must be consciously and deliberately undertaken. It does not matter if at the present moment external facts deny the truth of your assumption, if you persist in your assumption it will become a fact.

Signs follow, they do not precede.

To assume a new concept of yourself is to that extent to change your inner talking or Word of God and is, therefore, putting on the New Man. Our inner talking, though unheard by others, is more productive of future conditions than all the audible promises and threats of men. Your ideal is waiting to be incarnated, but unless you yourself offer it human parentage it is incapable of birth. You must define the person you wish to be and then assume the feeling of your wish fulfilled in faith that that assumption will find expression through you.

The true test of religion is in its use, but men have made it a thing to defend. It is to you that the words are spoken, "Blessed is she that believed, for there shall be an accomplishment of those things which were spoken unto her from the Lord."

Test it. Try it. Conceive yourself to be one that you want to be and remain faithful to that conception, for life here is only a training ground for image making. Try it and see if life will not shape itself on the model of your imagination.

Everything in the world bears witness of the use or misuse of man's inner talking. Negative inner talking, particularly evil and envious inner talking, are the breeding ground of the future battlefields and penitentiaries of the world. Through habit man has developed the secret affection for these negative inner conversations. Through them he justifies failure, criticizes his neighbors, gloats over the distress of others, and in general pours out his venom on all. Such misuse of the Word perpetuates the violence of the world.

The transformation of self requires that we meditate on a given phrase, a phrase which implies that our ideal is realized, and inwardly affirm it over and over and over again until we are inwardly affected by its implication, until we are possessed by it. Hold fast to your noble inner convictions or "conversations."

Nothing can take them from you but yourself. Nothing can stop them from becoming objective facts. All things are generated out of your imagination by the Word of God, which is your own inner conversation. And every imagination reaps its own Words which it has inwardly spoken.

The great secret of success is a controlled inner conversation from premises of fulfilled desire. The only price you pay for success is the giving up of your former conversation which belongs to the Old Man, the unsuccessful man. The time is ripe for many of us to take conscious charge in creating heaven on earth. To consciously and voluntarily use our imagination, to inwardly hear and only say that which is in harmony with our ideal, is actively bringing heaven to earth.

Every time we exercise our imagination lovingly on behalf of another, we are literally mediating God to that one. Always use your imagination masterfully, as a participant, not an onlooker. In using your imagination to transform energy from the mental, emotional level to physical level, extend your senses - look and imagine that you are seeing what you want to see, that you are hearing what you want to hear, and touching what you want to touch. Become intensely aware of doing so. Give your imaginary state all the tones and feeling of reality. Keep on doing so until you arouse within yourself the mood of accomplishment and the feeling of relief.

This is the active, voluntary use of the imagination as distinguished from the passive, involuntary acceptance of appearances. It is by this active, voluntary use of the imagination that the Second Man, the Lord from heaven, is awakened in man.

Men call imagination a plaything, the "dream faculty." But actually it is the very gateway of reality.

Imagination is the way to the state desired, it is the truth of the state desired, and the life of that state desired. Could you realize this fully, then would you know that what you do in your imagination is the only important thing. Within the circle of our imagination the whole drama of life is being enacted over and over again. Through the bold and active use of the imagination we can stretch out our hand and touch a friend ten thousand miles away and bring health and wealth to the parched lips of his being. It is the way to everything in the world. How else could we function beyond our fleshly limitations? But imagination demands of us a fuller living of our dreams in the present.

Through the portals of the present the whole of time must pass. Imagine elsewhere as here, and then as now. Try it and see. You can always tell if you have succeeded in making the future dream a present fact by observing your inner talking. If you are inwardly saying what you would audibly say were you physically present and physically moving about in that place, then you have succeeded. And you could prophesy it from these inner conversations, and from the moods which they awaken within you, what your future will be.

For one power alone makes a prophet - 'imagination', the divine vision. All that we meet is our Word made visible. And what we do not now comprehend is related by affinity to the unrecognized forces of our own inner conversations and the moods which they arouse within us.

If we do not like what is happening to us, it is a sure sign that we are in need of a change of mental diet. For man, we are told, lives not by bread alone but by every Word that proceeds from the mouth of God. And having discovered the mouth of God to be the mind of man, a mind which lives on Words or inner talking, we should feed into our minds only loving, noble thoughts. For with Words or inner talking we build our world.

Let love's lordly hand raise your hunger and thirst to all that is noble and of good report, and let your mind starve e'er you raise your hand to a cup love did not fill or a bowl love did not bless. That you may never again have to say,

"What have I said? What have I done, O All Powerful Human Word?"

Awakened Imagination

As you have heard, this morning's subject is "Awakened Imagination". It is my theme for the entire series of nineteen lectures. Everything is geared towards the awakening of the imagination. I doubt if there is any subject on which clear thinking is more rare than the imagination. The word itself is made to serve all kinds of ideas. many of them directly opposed to one another. But here this morning I hope to convince you that this is the redeeming power in man. This is the power spoken of in the Bible as the Second Man. "the Lord from Heaven".

This is the same power personified for us as a man called Christ Jesus.

In the ancient text it was called Jacob, and there are numberless names in the Bible all leading up and culminating in the grand flower called Christ Jesus.

It may startle you to identify the central figure of the Gospels as human imagination, but I am quite sure before the series is over, you will be convinced that this what the ancients intended that we should know, but man has misread the Gospels as history and biography and cosmology, and so completely has gone asleep as to the power within himself.

Now this morning I have brought you the means by which this mighty power in us may be awakened. I call it the art of revision. I take my day and I review it in my mind's eye. I start with the first incident in the morning. I go through the day; when I come to any scene in my unfolding day that displeased me, or if it didn't displease me if it was not as perfect as I thought it could have been, I stop right there and I revise it. I re-write it, and after I have re-written it so that it conforms to the ideal I wished I had experienced, then I experience that in my imagination as though I had experienced it in the flesh. I do it over and over until it takes on the tone of reality, and experience convinces me that that moment that I have revised and relived will not recede into my past. It will advance into my future to confront me as I have revised it. If I do not revise it, these moments, because they never recede and they always advance, will advance to confront me perpetuating that strange, unlovely incident. But if I refuse to allow the sun to descend upon my wrath, so that at the end of a day I never accept as final the facts of the day, no matter how factual they are, I never accept them, and revising it I repeal the day and bring about corresponding changes in my outer world.

Now, not only will this art of revision accomplish my every objective, but as I begin to revise the day it fulfills its great purpose and its great purpose is to awaken in me the being that men call Christ Jesus, that I call my wonderful human imagination, and when it awakens it is the eye of God and it turns inward into the world of thought and there I see that what formerly I believed to exist on the outside really exists within myself. No matter what it is, I then discover that the whole of Creation is rooted in me and ends in me as I am rooted in and end in God. And from that moment on I find my real purpose in life and my real purpose is simply to do the will of Him that sent me, and the will of Him that sent me is this --that of all that he has given me I shall lose nothing but raise it up again.

And what did he give me? He gave me every experience in my life. He gave me you. Every man, woman and child that I meet is a gift to me from my Father, but they fell in me because of my attitude towards society, because of my attitude towards myself. When I begin to awaken and the eye opens and I see the whole is myself made visible, I then must fulfill my real purpose, which is the will of Him that sent me, and the Will is to raise up those that I allowed in my ignorance when I slept to descend within me.

Then starts the real art of revision; to be the man, regardless of your impressions of that man, regardless of the facts of the case that are all staring you in the face, it is your duty when you become awakened to lift him up within yourself and you will discover that he was never the cause of your displeasure. When you look at him and you are displeased, look within and you will find the source of the displeasure. It did not originate there.

Now let me give you a case history to illustrate this point. I know a few of you were at the banquet and maybe a few of you heard me last Thursday on T. V. but I doubt in this audience of say twenty-three or twenty-four hundred of us, that more than say a hundred and fifty heard it, and even if you heard it you can hear it time and time again for it is this, that if you hear it will cause you to act upon it because as I told you, and I think I did last Sunday, but if I didn't let me tell you now; if you attended the entire nineteen and you became saturated with all that I have to tell you, so that you had all the knowledge you think it takes to achieve your objectives, and you did not apply what you received, it would avail you nothing; but a little knowledge which you carry out in action, you will find to be far more profitable than much knowledge which you neglect to carry out in action. So by repeating this case history this morning, though say a hundred or two hundred of you have heard it, it will help you to remember you must do something about it.

This past May in New York City, there sat a lady who had been coming for years and I made a simple observation that people must become doers of the word and not mere hearers only. For if a man only hears it and never applies what he hears he will never really prove or disprove what he has heard; and then I told the story of a lady who had only heard me three or four times and how she transformed the life of another, and this lady hearing what one who came only three times and this miracle took place in her life, she went home determined that she would really apply what she had heard over the years, and this is what she did.

Two years before, after a violent quarrel, she was ordered out of her son's home by her daughter-in-law. Her son said "Mother, you need no proof from me that I love you: it's obvious: I think I have proven that every day of my life, but if that is Mary's decision, and I regret it, it must be my decision, for I love Mary and we live in the same house and it is our house: it is our little family, and I am sorry she feels this way about it, but you know these little things that culminate in an explosion as took place today. If that is her decision, it is mine". That was two years ago. She went home and she realized that night after night for over two years she had allowed the sun to descend upon her wrath. She thought of this wonderful family that she loved and felt herself ostracized from it, expelled from the home of her son. She did nothing about revising it and yet I had been talking revision to my New York audience for the past year.

This is what she did now. She knew the morning's mail brought nothing. This was a Wednesday night. There had been no correspondence in two years. She had sent her grandson at least a dozen gifts in the two years. Not one was ever acknowledged. She knew they had been received for she had insured many of them; so she sat down that night and mentally wrote herself two letters--one from her daughter-in-law, expressing a great kindness for her, saying that she had been missed in the home and asking her when she was coming to see them; then she wrote one from her grandson in which he said "Grandmother, I love you". Then came a little expression of thanks for the last birthday present, which was in April, and then came a feeling of sadness rather because he hadn't seen her and begging her to come and see him soon.

These two short notes she memorized and then, as she was about to sleep, she took her imaginary hands and held these letters and she read them mentally to herself until they woke in her the feeling of joy because she had heard from her family; that she was wanted once more. She read these letters over and over feeling the joy that was hers because she had received them and fell asleep in her project. For seven nights this lady read these two letters. On the morning of the eighth day she received the letter: on the inside there were two letters--one from her grandson and one from her daughter-in-law. These letters were identical with the letters she had mentally written to herself seven days before.

Where was the estrangement? Where was the conflict? Where was the source of the displeasure that was like a running sore over two years? When man's eye is opened he realizes all that he beholds, though it appears without, it is within--within one's own imagination, of which this world of mortality is but a shadow.

She gave me permission to tell that story. When I told it, and we came to the period of questions and answers, there was a strange reaction from that crowd. They wondered what joy life would hold for any of us if we had to write our own letters; if we had to do everything to ourselves that seemingly is done in joy; that seemingly is spontaneous coming from another; but I don't want to write myself a love letter from my wife, or my sweetheart or my friend. I want that one to feel this way towards me and to express it unknown to me that I may receive a surprise in life.

Well, I am not denying that sleeping man firmly believes that is the way things happen. When a man awakes he realizes that everything he encounters is apart of himself, and what he does not now comprehend, he knows, because the eye is opened, that it is related by affinity to some as yet unrealized force in his own being; that he wrote it but he has forgotten it, that he slapped himself in the face but he has forgotten it; that within himself he started the entire unfolding drama, and he looks out upon a world, and it seems strange to him, because most of us in our sleep are totally unaware of what we are doing from within ourselves.

What that lady did, every man and woman in this audience today can do. It will not take you years to prove it; what I tell you now may startle you; it may seem to be bordering on insanity for the insane believe in the reality of subjective states and the sane man only believes in what the senses will allow, what they will dictate, and I'm going to tell you when you begin to awake, you assert the supremacy of imagination and you put all things in subjection to it. You never again bow before the dictates of facts and accept life on the basis of the world without.

To you Truth is not confined by facts but by the intensity of your imagination. So here we find the embodiment of Truth, which I say is human imagination, standing in the world drama before the embodiment of reason personified as Pontius Pilate. And he is given the authority to question truth and they ask him, "What is the truth?" and Truth remains silent. He refuses to justify any action of his; he refuses to justify anything that was done to him, for he knows no man cometh unto me save I call him: no man takes away my life, I lay it down myself.

You didn't choose me, I have chosen you. For here is Truth seeing nothing hereafter in pure objectivity, but seeing everything subjectively related to himself and he the source of all the actions that take place within his world; so Truth remains absolutely silent and says nothing when reason questions him concerning the true definition of Truth. Because when the eye opens it knows that what is an idea to sleeping man is a fact to the awakened imagination, an objective fact, not an idea. I entertain the idea of a friend and I make some wonderful concept of him in my mind's eye and when I sleep it seems to be a wish, it seems to be the longing of my heart, but purely subjective, just an idea. And the eye within me opens, and he stands before me embodying the quality that I desired in my sleep to see him express. So what is an idea to sleeping man, the unawakened imagination, is an objective reality to awakened imagination.

Now, this exercise calls for, I would say, the active, voluntary use of imagination as against the passive, involuntary acceptance of appearances. We never accept as true and as final anything unless it conforms to the ideal we desire to embody within our world, and we do exactly what the grandmother did. But now we start it and we do it daily. You may get your results tomorrow; it may come the day after; it may come in a week, but I assure you they will come.

You do not need some strange laboratory, like our scientists, to prove or disprove this theory. Here in 1905 a young man startled the scientific world with his equation that no one could even test. It is said not six men lived who could understand his equation. It was 14 years later before Lord Rutherford could devise the means to test that equation and he found that it was true, not 100%, because he did not have the means at his hand to really give it a complete test. It was another 14 years before further tests could be made. And you know the results of that equation that Einstein gave us in 1905. For today man, not knowing the power of his own imagination, stands startled at the results of that unlocking of energy. But he was the man who said, and I put it in the first page of my new book--"Imagination is more important than knowledge"

That was Albert Einstein. Imagination is more important than knowledge. For if man accepts as final the facts that evidence bears witness to, he will never exercise this God-given means of redemption, which is his imagination.

Now I'm going to ask you to test this: you will not take the three weeks that I am here to prove it or disprove it, but the knowledge of it cannot prove itself, only the application of that knowledge can prove it or disprove it. I know from experience you cannot disprove it. Take an objective, take a job, take some conversation with your boss, take an increase in salary. You say well, the job doesn't allow it, or maybe the Union will not allow it. I don't care what doesn't allow it.

Yesterday morning's mail brought me one, where, in San Francisco, this captain, a pilot, and he writes me that I saw him backstage after one of my meetings, and there he said, "But Neville, you are up against a stone wall. I am a trained pilot; I have gone all over the world, all over the seven seas; I'm a good pilot and I love the sea, not a thing in this world I want to do but go to sea; yet they restrict me to certain waters because of seniority. No matter what argument I give them the Union is adamant and they have closed the book on my request." I said, "I don't care what they have done, you are transferring the power that rightfully belongs to God, which is your own imagination, to the shadow you cast upon the screen of space.

"So here, we are in this room; need it remain a room? Can't you use your imagination to call this a bridge. This is now a bridge and I am a guest on the bridge of your ship, and you are not in waters restricted by the Union; you are in waters that you desire to sail your ship. Now close your eyes and feel the rhythm of the ocean and feel with me and commune with me and tell me of your joy in first proving this principle. and secondly in being at sea where you want to be. He is now in Vancouver on a ship bringing a load of lumber down to Panama. He has a complete list that will take him through the year what this man has to do. He is going into waters legitimately that the Union said he could not go. This doesn't dispense with unions, but it does not put anyone in our place- -no one, kings, queens, presidents, generals, we take no one and enthrone him and put him beyond the power that rightfully belongs to God. So I will not violate the law but things will open that I will never devise.

I will sit in the silence and within myself I will revise the picture. I will hear the very man who told me "No, and that's final" and hear him tell me yes, and a door opens. I don't have to go and pull strings or pull any wires whatsoever. I call upon this wonderful power within myself, which man has forgotten completely because he personified it and called it another man, even though it is a glorious picture of a man but that is not the man: the real man is not in some other world. When religion speaks, if it's a real religion, it speaks not of another world; it speaks of another man that is latent but unborn in every man that has attunement with another world of meaning, so that man sat and he tuned in with another world of meaning and brought into being a power that he allowed to go to sleep because he read the laws of man too well. He accepted as final the dictate of facts for they read him the by-laws, they read him the laws of the Union. And here today he is flying the ocean as he wants to do it. The grandmother is no longer locked out from the home she loved, but she is in communion, but she was locked out by herself for two years. And he was locked out by himself for well over 18 months, and burning up day after day allowing the sun to descend upon his wrath when he had the power within himself and the key to unlock every door in the world.

I say to each and everyone of you I wouldn't take from you your outer comfort, your religion, for all these things are like toys for sleeping man, but I come to awaken within you that which when it awakes it sees an entirely different world. It sees a world that no man when he sleeps could ever see, and then he starts to raise within himself every being that God gave him; and may I tell you God gave you every man that walks the face of the earth. He also gave it for this purpose that nothing is to be discarded. Everyone in the world must be redeemed and your individual life is the process by which this redemption is brought to pass.

So we don't discard because the thing is unpleasant, we revise it; revising it we repeal it, and as we repeal it it projects itself on the screen of space bearing witness to the power within us, which is our wonderful human imagination. And I say human advisedly--some would have me say the word divine. The very word itself means nothing to man. He has pushed it off from himself completely and divorced himself from the thing that he now bows before and calls by other names. I say human imagination. As Blake said "Rivers, mountains, cities, villages all are human". When the eye opens you see them in your own bosom, in your own wonderful bosom they all exist, they are rooted there. Don't let them fall and remain fallen; lift them up for the will of my Father is this, that of all that he has given me I should lose nothing but raise it up again, and I raise it up every time I revise my concept of another and make him conform to the ideal image I myself would like to express in this world. When I do unto him what I would love the world to do unto me, and see in me I am lifting him up.

And may I tell you what happens to that man when he does it? First of all, he is already turned around within himself. He no longer sees the world in pure objectivity, but the whole world subjectively related to himself, and hang it upon himself. As he lifts it up do you know he blooms within himself. When this eye of mine was first opened I beheld man as the prophet saw him. I saw him as a tree walking: some were only like little antlers of a stag, others were majestic in their foliage, and all that were really awake were in full bloom. These are the trees in the garden of God. As told us in the old ancient way of revision in the 61st chapter of the Book of Isaiah---"Go and give beauty for ashes, go and give joy for mourning, give the spirit of praise for the spirit of heaviness, that they may become trees of righteousness, plantings to the glory of God."

That is what every man must do, that's revision. I see ash when the business is gone; you can't redeem it, you can't lift it up, conditions are bad and the thing has turned to ash. Put beauty in its place; see customers, healthy customers, healthy in finances, healthy in the attitude towards you, healthy in every sense of the word. See them loving to shop with you if you are a shopkeeper; if you are a factory worker, don't see anything laying you off, lift it up, put beauty in the place of ash, for that would be ash if you were laid off with a family to feed. If someone is mourning, put joy in the place of mourning; if someone is heavy of spirit, put the spirit of praise in place of the spirit of heaviness, and as you do this and revise the day you turn around, and turning around you turn up, and all the energies that went down when you were sound asleep and really blind now turn up and you become a tree of righteousness, a planting to the glory of God. For I have seen them walking this wonderful earth, which is really the Garden; we have shut ourselves out by our concept of self and we have turned down.

As told us in the Book of Daniel, we were once this glorious tree and it was felled to the very base, and what formerly sheltered the nations and fed the nations and comforted the bird and gave some comfort to the animals from the sun of the day, of the heat of the day; and suddenly some voice said from within, "Let it lie, let it remain as it is, but do not disturb the roots; I will water it with the dew of heaven and as I water it with the dew of heaven it will once more grow again, but this time it will consciously grow, it will know what it really is and who it is. In its past it was majestic but it had no conscious knowledge of its majesty, and I felled it- -that was the descent of man. And now, he will once more spring from within himself and he will be a tree walking, a glorious, wonderful tree.

Now to those who are sound asleep this may seem to you too startling: this may be just as startling as Einstein's equation was; that was startling too. But I tell you I've seen it and I see it--men are destined to be trees in the garden of God. They are planted on earth for a purpose and they don't always remain men, they are transformed as they turn in and turn up. This is the true meaning of the transfiguration. There is a complete metamorphosis taking place like the grub into the butterfly. You don't remain what you appear to be when man is asleep, and there is no more glorious picture in the world than to see this living animated human being, for every branch within him is represented by an extension of himself called another, and when he lifts the other up that branch not only comes into leafage but it blossoms and the living human blossoms that blossom upon the tree of man who awakens.

So that's my message for you this year; I'll give it to you to stir into being that which sleeps in you, for the son of God sleeps in man and the only purpose of being is to awaken him. So it is not to awaken this, nice as it appears to be, but this man of sense-is only a casing: it is called the first man, but the first shall be last and the last shall be first. So that which comes into being second, like Jacob coming second from his mother's womb, he takes precedence over his brother Esau who came first. Esau was the one like this, he was made of skin and hair, and Jacob was made a smooth skinned lad, but that one that comes second suddenly becomes the lord of all the nations and that one sleeps in every man born of woman, and it is the duty of a teacher or a true religion to awaken that man, not to talk of another world, not to make promises to be fulfilled beyond the grave, but to tell him as he awakens now he is in heaven and the kingdom is come now, this day, on earth. For as he awakens he revises his day and he repeals his day and projects a more beautiful picture onto the screen of space.

By Imagination We Become

How many times have we heard someone say, "Oh, it's only his imagination?" Only his imagination - man's imagination is the man himself. No man has too little imagination, but few men have disciplined their imagination. Imagination is itself indestructible. Therein lies the horror of its misuse. Daily, we pass some stranger on the street and observe him muttering to himself, carrying on an imaginary argument with one not present. He is arguing with vehemence, with fear or with hatred, not realizing that he is setting in motion, by his imagination, an unpleasant event which he will presently encounter.

The world, as imagination sees it, is the real world. Not facts, but figments of the imagination, shape our daily lives. It is the exact and literal minded who live in a fictitious world. Only imagination can restore the Eden from which experience has driven us out. Imagination is the sense by which we perceived the above, the power by which we resolve vision into being. Every stage of man's progress is made by the exercise of the imagination. It is only because men do not perfectly imagine and believe that their results are sometimes uncertain when they might always be perfectly certain. Determined imagination is the beginning of all successful operation. The imagination, alone, is the means of fulfilling the intention. The man who, at will, can call up whatever image he pleases is, by virtue of the power of his imagination, least of all subject to caprice. The solitary or captive can, by intensity of imagination and feeling, affect myriads so that he can act through many men and speak through many voices. "We should never be certain," wrote William Butler Yeats in his IDEAS OF GOOD AND EVIL, "that it was not some woman treading in the wine-press who began that subtle change in men's minds, or that the passion did not begin in the mind of some shepherd boy, lighting up his eyes for a moment before it ran upon its way."

Let me tell you the story of a very dear friend of mine, at the time the costume designer of the Music Hall in New York. She told me, one day, of her difficulty in working with one of the producers who invariably criticized and rejected her best work unjustly; that he was often rude and seemed deliberately unfair to her. Upon hearing her story, I reminded her, as I am reminding you, that men can only echo to us that which we whisper to them in secret. I had no doubt but that she silently argued with the producer, not in the flesh, but in quiet moments to herself. She confessed that she did just that each morning as she walked to work. I asked her to change her attitude toward him, to assume that he was congratulating her on her fine designs and she, in turn, was thanking him for his praise and kindness. This young designer took my advice and as she walked to the theater, she imagined a perfect relationship of the producer praising her work and she, in turn, responding with gratitude for his appreciation. This she did morning after morning and in a very short while, she discovered for herself that her own attitude determined the scenery of her existence. The behavior of the producer completely reversed itself. He became the most pleasant professional employer she had encountered. His behavior merely echoed the changes that she had whispered within herself. What she did was by the power of imagination. Her fantasy led his; and she, herself, dictated to him the discourse they eventually had together at the time she was seemingly walking alone.

Let us set ourselves, here and now, a daily exercise of controlling and disciplining our imagination. What finer beginning than to imagine better than the best we know for a friend. There is no coal of character so dead that it will not glow and flame if but slightly turned. Don't blame; only resolve. Life, like music, can by a new setting turn all its discords into harmonies. Represent your friend to yourself as already expressing that which he desires to be. Let us know that with whatever attitude we approach another, a similar attitude approaches us.

How can we do this? Do what my friend did. To establish rapport, call your friend mentally. Focus your attention on him and mentally call his name just as you would to attract his attention were you to see him on the street. Imagine that he has answered, mentally hear his voice – imagine that he is telling you of the great good you have desired for him. You, in turn, tell him of your joy in witnessing his good fortune. Having mentally heard that which you wanted to hear, having thrilled to the news heard, go about your daily task. Your imagined conversation must awaken what it affirmed; the acceptance of the end wills the means. And the wisest reflection could not devise more effective means than those which are willed by the acceptance of the end.

However, your conversation with your friend must be in a manner which does not express the slightest doubt as to the truth of what you imagine that you hear and say. If you do not control your imagination, you will find that you are hearing and saying all that you formerly heard and said. We are creatures of habit; and habit, though not law, acts like the most compelling law in the world. With this knowledge of the power of imagination, be as the disciplined man and transform your world by imagining and feeling only what is lovely and of good report. The beautiful idea you awaken in yourself shall not fail to arouse its affinity in others. Do not wait four months for the harvest. Today is the day to practice the control and discipline of your imagination. Man is only limited by weakness of attention and poverty of imagination. The great secret is a controlled imagination and a well sustained attention, firmly and repeatedly focused on the object to be accomplished. "

Now is the acceptable time to give beauty for ashes, joy for mourning, praise for the spirit of heaviness; that they might be called trees of righteousness, the planting of the Lord that He might be glorified."

Now is the time to control our imagination and attention. By control, I do not mean restraint by will power but rather cultivation through love and compassion. With so much of the world in discord we cannot possibly emphasize too strongly the power of imaginative love. Imaginative Love, that is my subject next Sunday morning when I shall speak for Dr. Bailes while he is on his holiday. The services will be held as always at the Fox Wilshire Theater on Wilshire Boulevard, near La Cienega at 10:30. "As the world is, so is the individual," should be changed to, "As the individual is so is the world." And I hope to be able to bring to each of you present the true meaning of the words of Zechariah, "Speak ye every man the truth to his neighbor and let none of you imagine evil in your hearts against his neighbor."What a wonderful challenge to you and to me. "As a man thinketh in his heart so is he."As a man imagines so is he. Hold fast to love in your imagination. By creating an ideal within your mental sphere you can approximate yourself to this "ideal image" till you become one and the same with it, thereby transforming yourself into it, or rather, absorbing its qualities into the very core of your being. Never, never, lose sight of the power that is within you. Imaginative love lifts the invisible into sight and gives us water in the desert. It builds for the soul its only fit abiding place. Beauty, love and all of good report are the garden, but imaginative love is the way into the garden.

Sow an imaginary conversation, you reap an act;

Sow an act, you reap a habit;

Sow a habit, you reap a character;

Sow a character, you reap your destiny.

By imagination, we are all reaping our destinies, whether they be good, bad, or indifferent. Imagination has full power of objective realization and every stage of man's progress or regression is made by the exercise of imagination. I believe with William Blake, "What seems to be, is, to those to whom it seems to be, and is productive of the most dreadful consequences to those to whom it seems to be, even of torments, despair, and eternal death. By imagination and desire we become what we desire to be. Let us affirm to ourselves that we are what we imagine. If we persist in the assumption that we are what we wish to be, we will become transformed into that which we have imagined ourselves to be. We were born by a natural miracle of love and for a brief space of time our needs were all another's care. In that simple truth lies the secret of life. Except by love, we cannot truly live at all. Our parents in their separate individualities have no power to transmit life. So, back we come to the basic truth that life is the offspring of love. Therefore, no love, no life. Thus, it is rational to say that, "God is Love."

Love is our birthright. Love is the fundamental necessity of our life. "Do not go seeking for that which you are. Those who go seeking for love only make manifest their own lovelessness and the loveless never find love. Only the loving find love and they never have to seek for it."

Affirm the Reality of Our Own Greatness

In the creation of a new way of life, we must begin at the beginning, with our own individual regeneration. The formation of organizations, political bodies, religious bodies, social bodies is not enough. The trouble we see goes deeper than we perceive. The essential revolution must happen within ourselves. Everything depends on our attitude towards ourself – that which we will not affirm within ourself can never develop in our world. This is the religion by which we live, for religion begins in subjective experience, like charity, it begins at home. "Be ye transformed by the renewing of your mind" is the ancient formula and there is no other. Everything depends upon man's attitude toward himself. That which he cannot or will not claim as true of himself can never evolve in his world. Man is constantly looking about his world and asking, "What's to be done? What will happen?" when he should ask himself "Who am I? What is my concept of myself?" If we wish to see the world a finer, greater place, we must affirm the reality of a finer, greater being within ourselves. It is the ultimate purpose of my teaching to point the road to this consummation. I am trying to show you how the inner man must readjust himself – what must be the new premise of his life, in order that he may lose his soul on the level he now knows and find it again on the high level he seeks.

It is impossible for man to see other than the contents of his own consciousness, for nothing has existence for us save through the consciousness we have of it. The ideal man is always seeking a new incarnation but unless we, ourselves, offer him human parentage, he is incapable of birth. We are the means whereby the redemption of nature from the law of cruelty is to be effected. The great purpose of consciousness is to effect this redemption. If we decline the burden and point to natural law as giving us conclusive proof that redemption of the world by imaginative love is something that can never come about, we simply nullify the purpose of our lives through want of faith. We reject the means, the only means, whereby this process of redemption must be effected.

The only test of religion worth making is whether it is true born –

whether it springs from the deepest conviction of the individual, whether it is the fruit of inner experience. No religion is worthy of a man unless it gives him a deep and abiding sense that all is well, quite irrespective of what happens to him personally. The methods of mental and of spiritual knowledge are entirely different, for we know a thing mentally by looking at it from the outside, by comparing it with other things by analyzing and defining it. Whitehead has defined religion as that which a man does with his solitude. I should like to add, I believe it is what a man is in his solitude. In our solitude we are driven to subjective experience. It is, then, that we should imagine ourselves to be the ideal man we desire to see embodied in the world. If, in our solitude, we experience in our imagination what we would experience in reality had we achieved our goal, we will in time, become transformed into the image of our ideal. "Be renewed in the spirit of your mind – put on the new man – speak everyman truth with his neighbor." The process of making a "Fact of being a fact of consciousness" is by the "renewing of our mind." We are told to change our thinking. But we can't change our thought unless we change our ideas. Our thoughts are the natural outpouring of our ideas, and our innermost ideas are the man himself. The end of longing is always to be – not to do. Be still and know "I am that which I desire." Strive always after being. External reforms are useless if your heart is not reformed. Heaven is entered not by curbing our passions; but rather, by cultivating our virtues. An old idea is not quickly forgotten, it is crowded out by new ideas. It disappears when a wholly new and absorbing idea occupies our attention. Old habits of thinking and feeling – like dead oak leaves – hang on till they are pushed off by new ones. Creativeness is basically a deeper receptiveness, a keener susceptibility. The future dream must become a present fact in the mind of anyone who would alter his life. Every great out-picturing is preceded by a period of profound absorption. When that absorption is filled with our highest ideal, – when we become that ideal – then we see it manifest in our world and we realize that the present does not recede into the past, but advances into the future. This is essentially how we change our future. A "now" which is "elsewhere" has for us no absolute meaning. We only recognize "now" when it is at the same time "here." When we feel ourselves into the desired state "here" and "now" we have truly changed our future. It is this "Changing Your Future" which I hope to explain to you fully next

Sunday morning when I am speaking for Dr. Bailes at 10:30 at the Fox Wilshire Theater on Wilshire Boulevard near La Cienega. It is my purpose to stir you to a higher concept of yourself and to explain so clearly the method by which you can achieve this concept that each one of you will leave the service on Sunday morning a transformed being.

Discouraged people are sorely in need of the inspiration of great principles. We must get back to first principles if we are to speak with a voice that will kindle the imagination and rouse the spirit. Again, I must repeat, in the creation of a new way of life, we must begin at the very beginning with our own individual regeneration. Man's chief delusion is his conviction that he can do anything. Everyone thinks he can do – everyone wants to do and all ask, "What to do?" What to do? It is impossible to do anything. One must be. It is hard for us to accept the fact that "We, of ourselves, do nothing." It is especially difficult because it is the truth and the truth is always difficult for man to accept. But, actually, nobody can do anything. Everything happens – all that befalls man – all that is done by him – all that comes from him – all this happens, and it happens in exactly the same way that rain falls – as a result of a change in the temperature in the higher regions of the atmosphere. This is a challenge to us all. What concept are we holding of ourselves in the higher regions of our soul?

Everything depends upon man's attitude towards himself. That which he will not affirm as true within himself can never develop in his world. A change of concept of self is the right adjustment – the new relationship between the surface and the depth of man. Deepening is, in principle, always possible, for the ultimate depth lives in everyone, and it is only a question of becoming conscious of it. Life demands of us the willingness to die and to be born again. This is not meant that we die in the flesh. We die in the spirit of the old man to become the new man, then we see the new man in the flesh. "Subjection to the will of God" is an old phrase for it and there is, I believe, no new one that is better. In that self-committal to the ideal we desire to express, all conflict is dispersed and we are transformed into the image of the ideal in whom we rest. We are told that the man without a wedding garment reaches the Kingdom by cleverly pretending. He does not believe internally what he practices externally. He appears good, kind, charitable. He uses the right words, but inwardly he believes nothing. Coming into the strong light of those far more conscious than himself, he ceases to deceive. A wedding garment signifies a desire for union. He has no desire to unite with what he teaches, even if what he teaches is the truth. Therefore, he has no wedding garment. When we are united with the truth, then we will put off the old nature and be renewed in the spirit of our mind.

Truth will strip the clever pretenders of their false aristocracy. Truth, in its turn, will be conquered and governed by the aristocracy of goodness, the only unconquerable thing in the world.